SUNRISE

D0500126

All About Ants

All About
Ants

By Sue Whiting

NATIONAL GEOGRAPHIC

WASHINGTON D.C.

One of the world's largest nonprofit scientific and educational organizations, the National Geographic Society was founded in 1888 "for the increase and diffusion of geographic knowledge." Fulfilling this mission, the Society educates and inspires millions every day through its magazines, books, television programs, videos, maps and atlases, research grants, the National Geographic Bee, teacher workshops, and innovative classroom materials. The Society is supported through membership dues, charitable gifts, and income from the sale of its educational products. This support is vital to National Geographic's mission to increase global understanding and promote conservation of our planet through exploration, research, and education.

For more information, please call
1-800-NGS-LINE (647-5463) or write to the following address:
National Geographic Society
1145 17th Street N.W.
Washington, D.C. 20036-4688
U.S.A.

For information about special discounts for bulk purchases, please contact
National Geographic Books Special Sales at ngspecsales@ngs.org

Visit the Society's Web site: www.nationalgeographic.com

Published by National Geographic Society. Washington, D.C. 20036

Design by Project Design Company

Printed in the United States

Library of Congress Cataloging-in-Publication Data

Whiting, Sue.
    All about ants / by Sue Whiting.
        p. cm. -- (National Geographic science chapters)
    Includes bibliographical references and index.
    ISBN-13: 978-0-7922-5948-0 (library binding)
    ISBN-10: 0-7922-5948-3 (library binding)
    1. Ants. I. Title. II. Series.
    QL568.F7W626 2006
    595.79'6--dc22

2006016316

Photo Credits

Front Cover: © Hans Christian Heap/ Taxi/ Getty Images; Spine: © George Grall/ National Geographic Image Collection; Endpaper: © George Grall/ National Geographic Image Collection; 2-3: © Philip Chapman/Taxi/ Getty Images; 6: © Karen Tweedy-Holmes/ Australian Picture Library/ Corbis; 8: © Densey Clyne; 10-11: © APL/ Minden Pictures; 13: © Denis Crawford; 16: © Wolfgang Kaehler; 17: Christoph Burki/ Stone/ Getty Images; 18: © Densey Clyne ©; 19: © Densey Clyne; 20: © Mark Moffet/ Minden Pictures; 21: © Daniel Heuclin/ NHPA; 22: © APL/ Corbis; 23: © Densey Clyne; 26: © Ed Degginger; 27: © Tim Heneghan/ Index Stock; 28-29: © Animals Animals; 29 (bottom): © Mark Moffet/ Minden Pictures; 30: © Stephen Krasemann/ NHPA; 31 (top): © Stephen Krasemann/ NHPA; 32: Martin Dohrn/ naturepl.com; 33: © Dennind Matthews/ ANT Photo Library; 34: © Reg Morrison. Auscape; 35 (top): © Malcolm Cross; Illustrations by Dimitrios Prokopis.

Contents

A trail of ants searches
for food among the leaves
on the forest floor.

Ants Everywhere!

Ants have lived on Earth for over 100 million years. They live in nearly every part of the world. These six-legged creatures can be found in hot deserts, steamy tropical jungles, and even where there's snow and ice. There are over 10,000 different kinds of ants. Most are brown or black, but some are red, yellow, or green. These tiny insects vary in size and behavior, too. Despite their differences, all ants share some basic characteristics.

▶ Weaver ants are a pale yellow color.

Some ants make nests out
of leaves and twigs.

Chapter 1

Active Ants

Ants are social insects. They live and work together in large groups called colonies. The ants in a colony depend on each other so much that an individual ant cannot survive on its own outside the colony. The queen is the most important ant in the colony. Female worker ants and male ants called drones live in the colony, too.

These mounds lead to underground ant nests.

Most ant colonies live in nests. Different kinds of ants build their nests in different places. Some ants build their nests under the ground. Other ants build their nests in small piles of dirt, leaves, or twigs. Weaver ants build their nests in trees.

Since ants live together, they need to be able to communicate with each other. Ants communicate using scents called

Ants communicate using their sense of smell.

pheromones. They give off different scents to communicate different messages. Other ants detect the scents with their antennae.

If an ant is in danger it will give off a specific pheromone, alerting the other ants in the colony to be on guard. When an ant finds food, it will leave a scent trail showing the way to the food. Other ants will then follow the trail.

Ants made these anthills in Africa.

Chapter 2

Inside the Nest

An ant's nest is its home. Just like your home, an ant's nest has different rooms. Ants use the rooms for different things.

The oval-shaped rooms in the nest are called "chambers." Each chamber has holes to let air in. The queen ant lives in one chamber. Food is stored in several chambers. Other chambers are used as nurseries for eggs. Long tunnels join the chambers together.

An ant guards the entrance to its nest.

An Ant's Nest

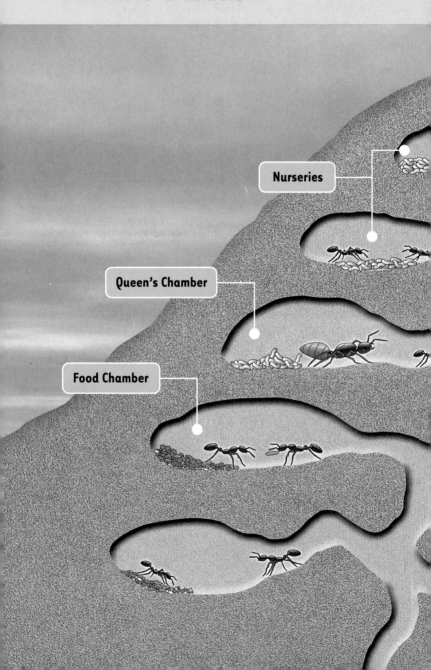

Nurseries

Queen's Chamber

Food Chamber

Sleeping Chamber

The worker ants are digging a new room.

Ants built this large nest
out of leaves.

Ants at Work

Ants hurry and scurry all over an anthill. What are they doing? The ants are all very busy. These tiny insects are hardworking and well organized. Each ant has a special job. In every colony, ants are divided into three groups: queens, drones, and worker ants. They all work together so that their colony will survive. Even though most individual ants only live 45–60 days, an ant colony can survive up to 30 years.

▶ Ants work to move a leaf.

The Queen

How would you like to lie around all day with your every need taken care of? Well, that's the life the queen ant enjoys. There is usually only one queen in each colony. She is the largest ant in the colony. Her job is to lay eggs.

A queen ant can live as long as 30 years.

A queen ant is the only ant that lays eggs.

When a queen ant is born, she has wings. The newly hatched queen ant flies away from the nest to look for a mate. When she is ready to lay her eggs, the queen looks for a good place for a nest. Then she breaks off her wings and digs a small tunnel. She lays her eggs inside the tunnel, starting a new colony. The eggs that hatch will build the nest and do the work of the colony.

A worker ant gathers food for the colony.

Worker Ants

The ants you see around the garden or in your house are the worker ants. They are smaller than the queen. They don't have wings. Worker ants are always female, but they can't lay eggs.

Worker ants are the busiest of all the ants. They do all the work for the colony. Luckily, there are thousands of worker ants in each colony. Each ant has a specific job to do.

Worker ants clean the queen.

Some worker ants feed the colony. They gather food and bring it back to the nest. Worker ants can carry loads that are more than ten times their own weight.

Some worker ants look after the queen. Their job is to feed her and keep her safe. Other worker ants take care of the nest. These ants keep the nest clean. They also build new chambers and tunnels.

Worker ants take care of the cocoons.

Some worker ants are like nurses. Their
job is to look after the eggs. These ants lick
the eggs to keep them clean. Soon larvae
hatch out of the eggs. The larvae look like
tiny white worms, but they are baby ants.
The larvae don't have legs and they don't
move around much on their own. Worker
ants spit up food to feed the larvae. Then the
larvae spin cocoons around themselves.
Inside the cocoons, the larvae will change
into adult ants.

Drones

Male ants are called drones. When they hatch out of their cocoons, drones are bigger than worker ants. They also have wings. Drones, like queens, have only one job to do. That job is to mate with the new queen. After mating, the male ants die. But new ant colonies are born.

Male ants fly from the nest to find mates.

Chapter 4

Amazing Ants

There are more than 10,000 different kinds of ants around the world. Not all ants live in the same kind of nests or eat the same food. But all ants live in colonies. Some of the more unusual colonies are really amazing. Let's take a look at a few and see how they are alike and different.

▲ A honey ant gathers honeydew off a leaf.

◀ A team of weaver ants attack and kill a larger ant.

Carpenter Ants

Carpenter ants make their nests in wood. They dig into the wood to carve out tunnels and chambers. These ants don't eat the the sawdust they create. They carry it outside the nest. The walls inside the nest are clean and smooth.

Most of the time carpenter ants make their nests in trees and logs. Sometimes carpenter ants find their way into houses. They like damp places like kitchens and bathrooms. Carpenter ants can do a lot of damage to a house. The wooden floors and doorways of houses can be destroyed.

▶ Carpenter ants make their nests in wood.

◀ This pile of sawdust came from the nest carpenter ants made in this doorway.

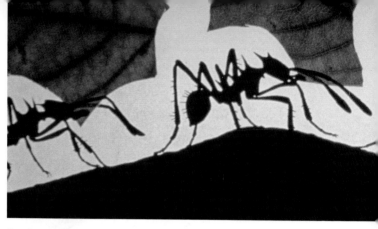

Leaf-cutter ants carry leaves back to the nest.

Leaf-Cutter Ants

Leaf-cutter ants are farmers. They farm fungus, which is like the mold that you see on an old piece of bread or fruit. Leaf-cutter ants feed their colonies with the fungus they grow.

Leaf-cutter ants are mostly found in hot, steamy parts of Central and South America. The ants leave the nest in search of juicy, green leaves. They use their sharp saw-toothed jaws to slice the leaves into small pieces. Sometimes leaf-cutter ants cut all of the leaves from a tree!

► Leaf-cutter ants have sharp saw-toothed jaws.

Once the leaf is cut, the leaf-cutter ant lifts it overhead and takes it back to the nest. The ants look like they are carrying little green umbrellas.

Inside the nest, other ants work like gardeners. They lick the leaves clean. Then the ants chew the leaves into a squishy pulp. The pulp is poked into the chamber that is the fungus garden. Fungus grows quickly on the leaf pulp. All the ants in the colony then eat the fungus.

Army Ants

Army ants march through the jungles of South America and Africa. Unlike other types of ants, army ants travel long distances to find food. They move in long, thick columns through the jungle.

An army ant colony can travel over large areas of jungle in a day. The ants will eat any small creature in their path. They can eat a mouse in a few minutes.

▲ Army ants eat a katydid.

◀ Army ants march in a column through the jungle.

Army ants make their nests by piling on top of each other.

Army ants make unusual nests. They don't dig or build nests like other ants. Their nest is made out of army ants! They cling to each other and make walls and tunnels and chambers. They surround the queen, her eggs, and the larvae. When the larvae are ready to hatch, the nest breaks up. The colony is on the move again!

Honeypot Ants

Honeypot ants are found in dry, warm areas of the world, including parts of North America, Africa, and Australia. Honeypot ants have found an amazing way to store food. Special worker ants store food in their stomachs. These worker ants are called repletes, which means they are full of food.

This honeypot ant's stomach is full of food.

Repletes hang in a chamber.

Worker ants collect food for the repletes to eat. The repletes' stomachs become very large and round because they eat so much. They become so full and heavy that they can't move. The repletes hang from the walls of chambers deep in the nest. When other sources of food are scarce, the other ants rub the repletes. This causes the repletes to spit up drops of food for the other ants to eat.

The Amazing World of Ants

Ants are amazing social insects. Colonies of hundreds of thousands of ants can survive because each ant has a special job to do. Whether a queen, a drone, or a worker ant, each ant is important. By working together these industrious insects can build a nest and help their colony grow.

What ants can you find where you live?

How to Write an A+ Report

1. Choose a topic.
- Find something that interests you.
- Make sure it is not too big or too small.

2. Find sources.
- Ask your librarian for help.
- Use many different sources: books, magazine articles, and websites.

3. Gather information.
- Take notes. Write down the big ideas and interesting details.
- Use your own words.

4. Organize information.
- Sort your notes into groups that make sense.

- Make an outline. Put your groups of notes in the order you want to write your report.

5. Write your report.

- Write an introduction that tells what the report is about.

- Use your outline and notes as you write to make sure you say everything you want to say in the order you want to say it.

- Write an ending that tells about your report.

- Write a title.

6. Revise and edit your report.

- Read your report to make sure it makes sense.

- Read it again to check spelling, punctuation, and grammar.

7. Hand in your report!

Glossary

chamber	a room inside an ant's nest
cocoon	a silky covering that an ant larva spins around itself
colony	a large group of ants that live and work together
drone	a male ant
fungus	a kind of mold
larva	a wormlike baby that hatches out of an ant egg
nursery	the area in the nest where the eggs are cared for
pheromone	the scent given off by ants to pass on messages to other ants
pulp	chewed-up and squishy leaves
queen	the largest ant in a colony and the only ant that lays eggs
replete	a kind of honeypot worker ant that stores food in its stomach
social insects	insects that live and work together

Further Reading

• Books •

Insects (First Pocket Guide Series). Washington, DC: National Geographic Society, 2001. Ages 8-10, 80 pages.

Johnson, Jinny. Simon and Schuster's Children's Guide to Insects and Spiders. New York, NY: Simon & Schuster Children's Publishing, 1997. Ages 9-12, 64 pages.

Julivert, Angels. The Fascinating World of Ants. Hauppauge, NY: Barron's Educational Series, 1991. Ages 9-12, 32 pages.

Mound, Laurence. Insect (Eyewitness Books). New York, NY: DK Publishing, Inc., 2004. Ages 9-12, 72 pages.

Wilsdon, Christina. National Audubon Society First Field Guide: Insects. New York, NY: Scholastic, 1998. Ages 9-12, 160 pages.

Winner, Cherie. Everything Bug: What Kids Want to Know About Insects and Spiders (Kids Faq's). Charlottesville, VA: Northwood Press. 2004. Ages 9-12, 64 pages.

• Websites •

Encarta Encyclopedia
http://encarta.msn.com/encyclopedia_761556353_3/Ant.html

Life Studies Online
http://www.infowest.com/life/aants.htm

South Dakota Department of Education
http://doe.sd.gov/octa/ddn4learning/themeunits/Ants/index.htm

ThinkQuest
http://library.thinkquest.org/C004404/hist.htm

Wikipedia: Online Encyclopedia
http://en.wikipedia.org/wiki/Ants

Index